Pot Pourri

& Other Secrets from the Garden

Pot Pourri

& Other Secrets from the Garden

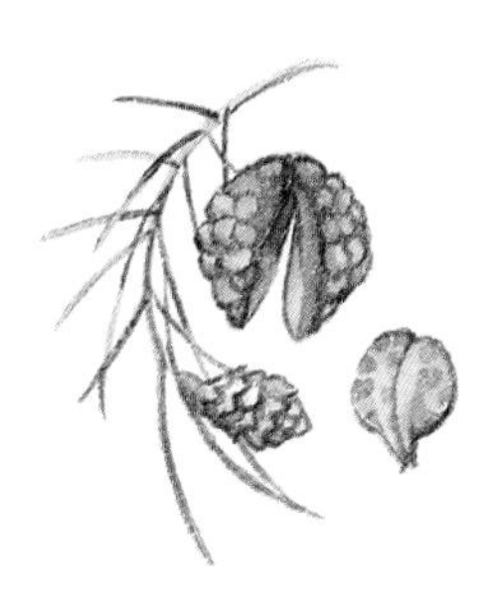

Written by Lynette Silver
Illustrated by Penny Walton

BANTAM BOOKS
SYDNEY • AUCKLAND • TORONTO • NEW YORK • LONDON

Pot Pourri & Other Secrets from the Garden

A Bantam Book

Prepared by Sally Milner Publishing Pty Ltd
First published in paperback in Australia and New Zealand in 1992 by Bantam.
Hardcover edition first published in 1995 by Bantam

National Library of Australia
Cataloguing-in-Publication Entry

Silver, Lynette Ramsay, 1945-
Pot pourri & other secrets from the garden.

ISBN 1 86359 344 6.

1. Potpourris (Scented floral mixtures). I. Title.
II. Title: Potpourri and other secrets from the garden.
745.92

Bantam Books are published by

Transworld Publishers (Aust.) Pty Limited
15-25 Helles Avenue, Moorebank, NSW 2170

Transworld Publishers (NZ) Limited
3 William Pickering Drive, Albany, Auckland

Transworld Publishers (UK) Limited
61-63 Uxbridge Road, Ealing, London W5 5SA

Bantam Doubleday Dell Publishing Group Inc.
1540 Broadway, New York, New York 10036

Illustrations by Penny Walton
Design by Wing Ping Tong
Typeset in Australia by Asset Typesetting Pty Ltd
Printed in Singapore

Contents

Acknowledgements	vi
Introduction	1
Making Pot Pourri	6
The Base Material	9
Making Pot Pourris without Fragrant Oil	27
Making Pot Pourri using Fragrant Oil	32
Pot Pourri Jars and Pots	47
Pomanders and Sachets	52
Other Nice-Smelling Things	69

Acknowledgements

The author is indebted to the staff of The Fragrant Garden, Erina, NSW, for the generous advice and assistance they have given me, and to perfumer Anne Hansen of The Olde Victorian Still Room, Prospect, SA, whose assistance in adapting pot pourri methods and recipes to suit local conditions was greatly appreciated.

Introduction

Imagine what a dull place our world would be if plants and trees and flowers had no scent at all. There would be no tangy smell from gum trees as we walked through the bush, no fresh, clean aroma as we crunched over needles in pine forests or chopped lemons in the kitchen, and not the faintest hint of sweet-smelling roses or newly-cut grass wafting on the breeze on a warm summer evening.

Since ancient times, people have enjoyed the wonderful range of scents that nature provides. Thousands of years ago Egyptians, Greeks and Romans discovered the pleasure of bathing in scented water or massaging their bodies with perfumed oils. The Egyptians loved the sweet smell of roses so much that they preserved large pots of rose petals over the warmer months to make sure that they had plenty during winter when the bushes were no longer flowering.

As the world's population grew, fragrant herbs and spices, as well as flower petals, were in very great demand. Many of the herbs and spices were used to make medicines and ointments, or to flavour and preserve food. Others were very important in general health

care. Before people knew about germs and how sickness is spread, they believed that certain herbs and spices kept away diseases such as the dreaded Black Death (or Plague), which killed thousands of people every year for many centuries.

These herbs and spices would either be placed in large urns around the house, scattered on the floor, burnt to give off a strong scent or actually carried on a person's body. And, although they might seem strange, in many cases these methods actually worked. Some herbs are known to be able to kill or weaken

germs and are called 'antiseptic'. Others can act as an insect repellent to drive away disease-carrying flies, as well as fleas and mosquitoes which carry illnesses like plague and malaria.

Another use for natural fragrances was to take away or cover up bad household smells. Piped running water, flushing toilets and the sewerage system are all quite modern inventions. Not so long ago, houses were often built on the bare earth, with very few windows. Sewage flowed through the streets in open drains, which, as you can imagine, smelt awful and were very unhealthy.

To freshen the air, the servants or lady of the house would scatter pleasant smelling leaves and herbs on the floor and keep large pots of dried flower petals mixed with spices in each room so that the bad odours would be less noticeable. The French people called these fragrant pots *pots pourris* — the name that is still used today.

Funnily enough, *pot pourri* (pronounced po-poo-ri) originally came from the Spanish word for stew — *olla podrida.* It means 'rotten pot' and describes another way of making pot pourri, where the ingredients are actually allowed to 'go rotten'.

Because pot pourri made this way does not look at all attractive (although it smells

wonderful it looks like dried-out sludge), this book deals only with the more appealing and far more creative 'dry' method.

The idea of covering up stale and unpleasant smells also extended to people. Because they believed that to take a bath was life-threatening, and because many of the fancy and elaborate clothes of the day could not be washed (and drycleaning had not been invented), most people, as well as their houses, also smelt.

People were also terrified of catching a deadly disease. To solve both these problems they carried or wore 'pomanders'. These were either dried, spiced oranges or special little containers filled with fragrance mixed with a special substance called 'ambergris'. The name 'pomander' originally comes from the Latin words *pomum de ambra* meaning 'apple of ambergris'.

Many of the pomander containers were quite beautiful. Some were made of gold and silver and very rich people even had ground jewels added to the fragrant mixture. Fancy or plain, pomanders were popular with everyone. The scent wafting from them covered up stale body odour, helped to keep germs away and also made the stench from the rotting garbage that

littered the streets and the open drains less noticeable.

Since we are fortunate enough to live in a country where there is little disease, where garbage is collected regularly, where city streets are swept and where houses are properly built with good ventilation, running water and proper drains and toilets, we do not have to put up with the smells that were so common in past times. However, the art of making pot pourris and pomanders has not been lost, and we can still enjoy the lovely fragrances which people created in the past. Since this knowledge has been handed down, we can put these traditional crafts to good use — not to cover up bad odours or drive away disease, but to make beautifully scented pots, pomanders, bath oils and sachets purely for our own pleasure and enjoyment.

This book will show you how very easily you can use oranges and lemons, wood shavings from a workshop, flowers growing in your garden, leaves and seed pods collected from the countryside, herbs and spices from your kitchen, and, believe it or not, even ordinary weeds, to fill your home with wonderful and, more importantly, environmentally friendly scents which will delight.

Making Pot Pourris

Many traditional pot pourri recipes are quite complicated, needing large amounts of highly perfumed petals, as well as ingredients which are often difficult to find.

The pot pourris in this book are very easy to make. You will need only a few items of basic equipment, the dried base material (almost anything that grows in the garden or countryside), spices or perfumed (fragrant) oil, and a special ingredient called a 'fixative' to fix or hold the scent.

You will need

SCISSORS — a pair of round-ended scissors for snipping flowers, leaves and seed pods.

GLOVES — a pair of gardening gloves to protect your hands from prickles and spiky leaves.

CONTAINERS — a container, such as a basket or small bucket, for carrying the things you have collected, and containers in which to store your dried material until you are ready to begin making the pot pourri. Anything made from natural materials that will 'breathe' and keep out the dust will do, e.g. large paper bags, shoe

boxes, crockery pots or bowls. If you use a bowl, drape an old tea towel over the top to keep out the dust. We will also use these containers to mix and then store the finished pot pourris. Also any decorative containers that you can find, as long as they are not metal or plastic, for your finished pot pourris.

NEWSPAPER — sheets of newspaper for drying flowers and leaves.

MEASURING CUPS AND SPOONS — for measuring the amounts of herbs, petals and spices needed for each recipe.

EYE-DROPPER — An eye-dropper, if possible (for recipes needing a fragrant oil).

A WORD OF WARNING

Because Australia is a very hot place, it is very important that you choose a container for storing your pot pourri that will 'breathe'. Think what happens on a warm day if you are wearing clothes that do not let your skin breathe. Very soon you become sticky and sweaty. If your pot pourri is in a tightly lidded container that cannot breathe and if you have left any moisture in your dried mix, the heat will make your pot pourri sweat too. Instead of having a lovely fragrant mix, you will have a horrible, slimy, mouldy mess.

Although you *can* use your pot pourri straight-away, most pot pourris, especially those made with fragrant oils, improve if they are left in the mixing/storing container for one or two weeks to allow the scents to blend properly.

The Base Material

The first ingredient you need is the base material — leaves, flowers, seed pods. The scent from some pot pourris does not come from the base material, but from a fragrant oil added later. If you are going to make a pot pourri that does not use a fragrant oil to provide the perfume, your base material will need to be scented.

If you are using a fragrant oil, it does not matter very much if the flowers and leaves you use are scented or not. The most important things for you to look for are **texture** and **colour**, which will help make your pot pourri attractive as well as interesting.

Do not worry if you do not have a garden of your own. Be on the alert for things you can use whenever you are out and about. As long as you dry them out thoroughly you can use flowers, leaves, seeds, seed pods, seed heads, citrus peel, bark, pine needles, small knobbly twigs, wood shavings, pine cones, grasses, bark chips, seaweed, sea shells and common weeds.

Gathering from the garden

The time to collect your base material from the garden is either in the morning, after the sun has dried all the overnight dew, or in the afternoon, before the evening dew settles. Carefully snip flowers from the plant with your scissors and place them in your basket or container. If you are collecting from prickly shrubs such as rose bushes or some of the Australian native plants, remember to wear gloves to protect your hands.

Unless you have a big garden, you will probably not be able to gather all your flowers at the one time. This is perfectly all right because once the petals have dried out they can be kept in the containers until you gather enough to make your pot pourri.

Leaves, as well as the flowers, from many plants dry well. If the leaves are very small, do not snip them off one by one but take a whole spray. They can then be dried on the stem.

Many shrubs whose flowers are small or not very attractive have leaves that have an interesting texture when dried. Others have a strong scent, such as a bushy herb called lemon verbena. Its lemony smell makes it very useful in spicy or citrus pot pourris.

Another plant with strong-smelling leaves is rosemary, a herb which is used to flavour many cooking dishes. Some Australians like to wear a sprig of rosemary, which means 'remembrance', on ANZAC Day.

To find out whether a leaf is scented, crush it between your fingers. If it smells nice, use it in your pot pourri.

Some of the plants found in many suburban gardens and from which you might like to collect flowers and leaves are:

Australian natives (for a list of suitable plants, see Gathering from the Bush section)

bougainvillea
calendulas
carnations
cassia
Chinese lantern
chrysanthemums
crepe myrtle
daffodils
daisies
delphiniums
fern
forget-me-not
freesias
gardenia
geraniums
gerberas
honeysuckle
hibiscus
hydrangeas
jacaranda (also the seed pods)
jasmine
jonquils
lavender
lemon
lemon verbena
lilac
marigolds
mock orange
nasturtium
orange
pansies
peach
pine needles and cones
poppies
rosemary
roses
stocks
sweet peas
sunflowers
violets
wallflowers
wisteria
zinnias

Gathering from the bush

If you enjoy walking in the bush, you will have great fun collecting the many things which can be found there. **Do not**, however, pick or remove *anything* when walking in a State Recreation Area or National Park as this is against the law and you will find yourself in trouble with the park rangers. These areas of land have been set aside for everyone to enjoy — and so have to be preserved for future generations. *All* plants (flora) and animals (fauna) in these parks are protected. Some plants, because of their rarity, are protected everywhere, not just in National Parks. Your state National Parks and Wildlife Service has a list of these plants — so it is wise to check with them before picking any plant you may not recognise. The ones on the protected list that you might know are flannel flowers, boronia, Christmas bells, some grevillea flowers, waratahs and many orchids and ferns, so don't pick any of those.

If you are especially interested in collecting scented leaves, the bush is the place to be, for there are many Australian natives with wonderfully fragrant leaves. Remember, if you want to know whether a shrub is scented, crush a couple of leaves between your fingers.

Before you set out on your bush walk, remember that it is important not to go alone or to stray off the track in case you get lost. It is also a sensible idea to wear strong shoes and socks and to keep an eye out for snakes, especially if the weather is warm.

When collecting from the bush, you will have to remember to look up, around and down since many things besides flowers and leaves are useful for pot pourris. Some, such as seed pods, sticks and bark, will be lying on the ground. Others you will have to snip off. Many native plants have very tough stems so don't forget your scissors! Never try to pull or twist off flowers, seedpods or greenery with your fingers — you will only end up damaging the plant.

As you walk through the bush, keep your eyes peeled for old banksia flowers. These look like the wicked 'banksia men' in the story books and at first glance do not seem very nice. However, the 'eyes' of the banksia men are really very interesting seed pods, and hidden underneath the hairy part (the old, dried stamens) is something very unexpected — a rich brown, velvety stick. To uncover the velvet you will need to remove the old stamens and also the outer coating of the stick. This rubs off quite easily to reveal the velvet beneath.

Also watch out for paperbark trees. These are quite common and have a bark that separates very easily into thin layers. If there is none lying on the ground, carefully peel small pieces from the tree, but do not take too

much bark from the one place or you might damage the tree.

Some of the more common native flowers, leaves and seed pods you might like to gather are:

- banksia pods (and the velvet sticks beneath)
- bracken
- bottlebrush (callistemon) leaves, flowers and seed pods
- cypress pine leaves and cones
- everlasting daisies
- gum tree (eucalyptus) leaves, nuts and bark
- hakea flowers, leaves and pods
- heath flowers
- kangaroo-paw
- lemon-scented myrtle leaves
- mint bush
- Mountain Devil pods
- native cassia
- native daisies
- native violets
- paperbark leaves and bark
- pittosporum flowers and leaves
- she-oak (casuarina) needles and nuts
- tea-tree flowers and leaves
- wattle flowers, leaves and seed pods
- white cedar flowers

Boronia, Christmas bush, flannel flowers, ferns and grevilleas are also very suitable for bush pot pourris. However the first three plants mentioned, plus some ferns and three varieties of grevillea, are protected. They *cannot* be

picked unless they are growing in private suburban gardens.

Gathering from the countryside and roadside

The countryside and roadside are wonderful places to find very interesting plants and weeds. Just about any grain that is grown by farmers, like wheat, oats and barley, has seeds and seed heads which can be used in pot pourris. Quite often, stalks of grain can be found growing alongside a country road, where seeds have fallen from passing trucks or been carried by birds. These give texture to a basic pot pourri mix. Some native grasses have beautiful feathery seed heads too.

Besides the weeds that grow in many gardens, there is also a great variety which can be collected in the countryside. These include clover flowers, Paterson's curse (also known as Salvation Jane), whose rich purple flowers dry very well, and lantana, a bushy plant with clusters of tiny, colourful flowers that are easy to gather.

Other weeds to watch for are blow fly (or bubble) grass, dandelion flowers and a yellow flowering plant called coreopsis (also known as calliopsis), which grows readily alongside

roads and railway tracks. There is a story that years ago, a lady who had settled in Australia missed the colourful wildflowers that grew along the roadside in her homeland so much that she decided to liven up the bush. Wherever she went, she scattered the seeds of the brightly coloured coreopsis flower.

Other materials you can collect

Other materials which are good to add to a pot pourri base are wood shavings, wood and bark chips, fruit seeds, nuts, dried fruit, citrus peel, seaweed, sea shells and kitchen herbs and spices.

Wood shavings and wood chips

Wood shavings are very useful as they are light yet large, and have a lovely curly shape. Some also have a beautiful scent. Any wood shavings will do and if you find the natural colour a little dull, you can easily dye the shavings with food colouring: just add a few drops to some water and dip the shavings in it. If they are too pale for your liking, add a few more drops of colour and dip them again.

Wood chips and some seed pods also dye well. Should you want a very strong shade you

can use the food colouring without adding water. If you decide to do this, it is best to use a small paint brush to apply the dye, otherwise your fingers will also change colour! Fluffy seed heads, clover flowers, blow fly grass, and many other weeds and grasses can also be dyed in the same way as wood shavings.

Fruit seeds and nuts

Next time you eat an apricot, peach, plum or mango, save the seed and dry it out. Small seeds, such as sunflower seeds and pumpkin kernels, and nuts, including almonds and hazelnuts, can be added to a basic mix, while the larger ones can be used to decorate the top of a pot pourri. Peach seeds, which have a lovely texture, are very attractive. Like wood chips, seeds can also be dyed different colours.

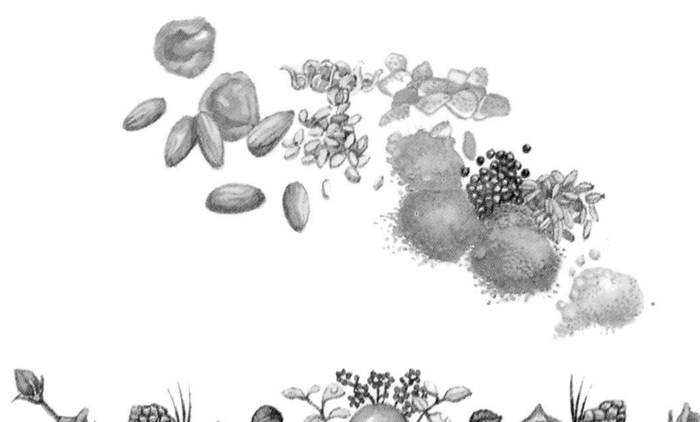

Dried fruit

Ordinary dried fruit, such as apple and apricot pieces, can be used to add colour and a fruity fragrance to a sweet, fruity or spicy pot pourri mix.

Citrus peel

The most common citrus fruits are oranges, mandarins, grapefruit, lemons and limes. The rind of each has a very distinctive smell and, when dry, can be added to almost any pot pourri. Next time you have a piece of citrus fruit, peel the rind off in very small, thin layers and save it. It is best to use an ordinary vegetable peeler to peel the fruit, not a knife. Try not to peel off any pith (the white part under the peel) as this can go mouldy.

Citrus peel adds colour and scent and also helps to hold the fragrance in the pot pourri. Mandarin and orange rinds are good to add to sweet or spicy pot pourri, while lemon, grapefruit and lime go well with either fresh or spicy scents.

Seaweed and sea shells

If you live near the beach, you might like to look for small pieces of seaweed and pretty shells. You will need to wash the seaweed quite a few times in fresh water to get rid of the salt, but once it is clean and thoroughly dry, it can be used in almost any type of pot pourri. Tiny pieces of driftwood washed up on the beach are also worth collecting.

Kitchen herbs and spices

You will often notice kitchen herbs and spices in pot pourri recipes. It is best to use fresh garden herbs (such as mint, rosemary, thyme, basil and oregano) which you have dried yourself, since many of the ready-dried shop variety have been powdered or chopped too finely. Because of their fresh smell, many herbs can be added to a bush pot pourri mix.

Since ground spices are fine and powdery they can give a dusty, unattractive look to a pot pourri. Wherever possible, try to use whole spices, such as pieces of cinnamon stick,

cracked nutmeg and whole or cracked cloves. Spices can be added to floral, spicy and bush pot pourris. They also help the pot pourri to hold its scent.

If your parents do not have herbs and spices in the garden or in the kitchen cupboard, do not worry. Small bunches of herbs can be bought from the greengrocer, while whole, dried spices can be found in any grocery or health food store.

HINT

To crush whole cloves or other hard spices, place them in a strong plastic or paper bag and hit them, not too heavily, with a hammer.

Drying your base material

Drying your base material is very important, for if you do not completely dry out your ingredients, your pot pourri could go mouldy. You will soon discover that some flowers and leaves dry more easily and keep their colour better than others. Experiment with as many flowers as possible to find those that look good when they are dried. You may get quite a few surprises. Heavily scented gardenia and frangipani flowers, which are beautiful when alive,

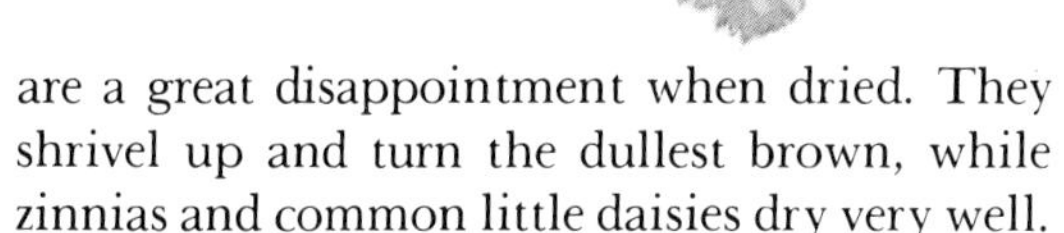

are a great disappointment when dried. They shrivel up and turn the dullest brown, while zinnias and common little daisies dry very well.

When you have gathered your flowers, you will have to decide whether you need to remove the petals first, so that they will dry properly or whether you can leave them as they are. Roses, carnations and marigolds, which are quite thick, fleshy flowers, need to have their petals removed, but simple, flatter flowers, such as daisies and pansies, as well as many of the Australian natives, do not.

To dry flowers and leaves, simply spread them out on a few sheets of newspaper in a warm, airy spot. Make sure that the spot you have chosen is not in the sunlight or the colours in the flowers will fade. Each day, toss

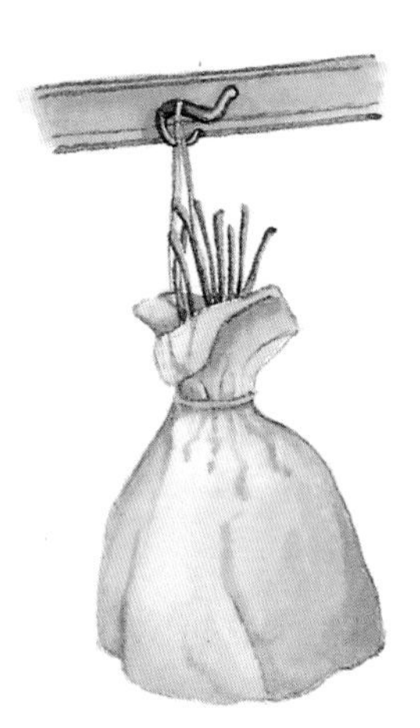

the petals and leaves with your fingers to make sure that they dry out evenly.

Drying leaves on the stalk is even easier. Tie the ends of one or two stalks together and then hang the bunch in a warm, airy place (such as from the rafters of the garage), until they have dried out. The leaves will then come away very easily from the stalk.

To dry and collect seeds from seed heads, place the seed head upside down in a paper bag, with its stalk poking out. Tie the top of the bag with string, catching the stalk, and hang it in a warm, airy place. After a few days, shake the bag. If they are dry, the seeds will fall from the seed head into the bag.

Unlike the other material you have collected, citrus peel should be dried in the sun on newspaper. Remember to turn the pieces over frequently so that they dry out thoroughly. After two days the peel should be rock hard.

When the flowers and leaves are ready, they should be crisp, but not too crisp, rather like slightly stale breakfast cereal. You will notice that when the leaves, flower petals and peel have dried, they will have shrivelled up quite a bit and are not nearly as heavy as they were, since almost all the moisture has evaporated.

Some plants, such as the natives, which do not have much moisture to begin with, will dry in two days. Others will perhaps take up to a week. Some might even dry out so crisply that they crumble to bits! Don't worry — it was better to find out beforehand that these materials are unsuitable than after you've made your pot pourri.

As soon as your base materials dry, store the pieces in containers until the rest are dry, or until you are ready to make your pot pourri.

The fixative

To stop the fragrance from your pot pourri evaporating too quickly, you must also use a fixative to 'fix' or keep the scent. In the past,

fixatives were obtained from sperm whales, musk deer and civet cats, which all had to be killed first. When people realised the importance of looking after our wildlife, the killing of these animals was stopped. (Remember what the word *pomander* meant in Latin? — apple of ambergris. Ambergris is a substance found in sperm whales which helps to fix perfume.)

Nowadays the fixatives used come from plants. The three which we will use are dried citrus peel, oakmoss (an attractive type of lichen that grows on trees), and orris root powder, which is a very fine powder made from the roots of an iris plant. Some spices also act as fixatives.

Where to get fixatives

You know how to dry citrus peel (see pages 19 and 24 if you have forgotten). Oakmoss and orris root powder can be bought from most craft shops and orris root can also be bought from some chemist shops. Although you can use either oakmoss or orris root powder in most of the recipes in this book, oakmoss is far more attractive and easier to handle than orris root powder, which tends to give pot pourris a dusty look.

Making Pot Pourris without Fragrant Oils

The basic recipe

This basic recipe, which does not need any fragrant oil, obtains its perfume from scented leaves and flowers and from the citrus peel and spices, which also act as fixative. You can make as much of the pot pourri as you like. The only thing to remember is that for every three cups of dry mix, you will need one cup of spices, about ½ cup of citrus peel and, if you want the scent to last longer, 1 cup of oakmoss or 1 tablespoon orris root powder.

What you need

3 cups of any dried, scented flowers and leaves
½-1 cup of any dried citrus peel
1 cup of mixed whole or cracked spices (such as cloves, cinnamon and nutmeg)
1 cup crumbled oakmoss or 1 tablespoon orris root powder (optional)

What to do

- Place the dried leaves and flowers in your container and gently shake or mix well.

- Add the citrus peel and gently shake or mix well.
- Add the spices and fixative and once more gently shake or mix well.
- Look inside the container. If the mixture looks too dull add some dried, colourful petals. These do not need to be scented.

- Put the mixture into decorative bowls. If you are not using the pot pourri straight away leave it in the container, which should then be covered and stored in a cool, dry place such as a cupboard. (If you are using a paper bag, fold over the top of the bag and secure it with a clothes peg or paper clip.) About twice a week, shake or stir the contents gently.

Other simple recipes

You might like to try these easy recipes. Just follow the directions given for the basic recipe.

Sweet Rose Pot Pourri

3 cups dried, scented rose petals
½-1 cup dried orange peel
1 cup of cracked cloves and cinnamon sticks
1 teaspoon nutmeg
1 cup crumbled oakmoss or 1 tablespoon orris root powder

You could also try using other sweet-smelling flowers — such as orange blossom, jasmine and lavender — either on their own or mixed.

ANZAC or Rosemary Pot Pourri

This simple pot pourri is a good one to place in the kitchen because it uses the herb rosemary. Its fragrance will last for perhaps five or six months.

4 cups dried rosemary leaves
2 cups dried lemon verbena
4 crushed cinnamon sticks
¼ cup crushed cloves
1½ cups crumbled oakmoss or 1½ tablespoons orris root powder

HINT
To make this pot pourri look more attractive, toss a few dried blue flowers through the mixture before putting it into an open bowl.

Lemony Pot Pourri

This is also a good pot pourri for the kitchen.

2 cups dried lemon verbena
about ½ cup dried lemon geranium leaves
½ cup dried lemon peel
½ cup dried orange peel
⅔ cup crumbled oakmoss or 3 teaspoons orris root powder

Herb Pot Pourri

2 cups dried rose petals
1 cup dried lavender
1 cup dried lemon verbena
1 cup any other lemon-scented leaves
½ cup dried rosemary
½ cup dried thyme
½ cup dried marjoram
¼ cup dried mint leaves
20 crushed cloves

1 crushed cinnamon stick
2 cups crumbled oakmoss or 2 tablespoons orris root powder

Minty Lemon Pot Pourri

1 cup dried lemon verbena
1 cup any other dried, lemon-scented leaves
1 cup dried mint
1 cup dried rose petals

Making Pot Pourris using Fragrant Oils

As you can see, many traditional pot pourri recipes need heavily scented flowers and herbs — plants that many people do not have growing in their gardens or in a large enough supply. This does not mean that if you don't have a garden, you cannot make pot pourri. Remember the perfumed oil in our basic list?

You can make a pot pourri from just about anything that grows, as long as you use a fragrant oil to supply the perfume. These oils are quite inexpensive to buy and come in a wide range of scents.

Although just one fragrant oil is probably enough to begin with, to have an oil from three or four 'fragrance families' would allow you to experiment. The six fragrance families which are most suitable for beginners are:

floral (such as rose, jasmine or lavender)
citrus (such as lemon or orange)
fruity (such as peach or strawberry)
spicy (such as cloves, cinnamon or a spicy mix)
woody (such as pine, cedar or sandalwood)
Australian bush (such as eucalyptus or lemon-scented gum)

How to choose which pot pourri to make

Before you gather your material for your basic mixture, it is a good idea to decide how you want your pot pourri to **look** and **smell**. The base is entirely up to you, but choose dry materials which go with the scent you have chosen. Also remember not to mix too many colours and textures, otherwise it might look a bit messy. Here are some tips which might help you.

Floral pot pourris

If you like sweet, flowery scents, it is probably best to use a mixture of flower petals and leaves,

with perhaps a few pretty, soft, seed pods for texture. Sweet whole spices such as cloves and cinnamon bark can be added. Red, pink and apricot colours go well with rose scents, while blues, lilacs, purple and pink are better suited to lavender.

Citrus pot pourris

For a citrus-scented pot pourri, try lemon-scented leaves, citrus leaves, citrus peel, orange or lemon blossoms, and perhaps a few wood shavings. The colours that go best with citrus scent are those found in citrus fruits — lemon, green, lime, yellow and orange.

Fruity pot pourris

These sweet-scented pot pourris could perhaps be made from a mixture of flowers, leaves, dried

fruit, soft seed pods and fruit seeds. Colours that go well with a peach fragrance are apricot, pink and green, while red, pink and green suit a strawberry-scented pot pourri.

Spicy and woody pot pourris

For spicy and woody pot pourris, experiment with coloured flowers, leaves, citrus peel, seed pods, nuts, wood shavings, small cones and whole spices. Spicy and woody fragrances are ones which most men like very much. Rich, earthy tones such as brown, orange, deep green and warm red, as well as softer yellows and greens suit this type of pot pourri.

Australian bush pot pourri

For a bush pot pourri, try a mixture of gum leaves, seed pods, small pieces of bark, native

flowers and perhaps one or two sticks of banksia velvet. If you want to dye any of the material, try to use the colours found in the bush — greens, lemons, browns, yellows and reds. Lemon and eucalyptus scents go well with a green and yellow bush mix, while a heavier, sweeter, spice fragrance is just right for a richly coloured pot pourri.

Remember, these are only suggestions. The important thing is to experiment and try out as many different combinations as possible so that *you* will be pleased with the result.

The basic recipe

As a general rule, these pot pourris need about four times as much dry mixture *by weight* as fixative. This means that for every 4 cups of light, dry mixture you will need to add 1 cup of oakmoss or 1 tablespoon of orris root powder. (As a rough guide, 4 cups of light, dry mixture weigh about 100 grams or about 4 ounces, and one cup of oakmoss or 1 tablespoon of orris root powder weighs about 25 grams or about 1 ounce.) Depending on the quality, ten drops (or about one capful) of fragrant oil will usually perfume 4 cups of dry mix.

What you need

3 or 4 cups of any dry mix that pleases you
1 cup crumbled oakmoss or 1 tablespoon orris root powder
10 drops of any fragrant oil to suit the mixture you have chosen

A WORD OF WARNING

If you double this recipe to make a larger pot pourri, *do not* double the amount of oil or the fragrance will be too strong. Just add a little at a time until it is strong enough.

What to do

- Place the dry mix in your container and either gently shake or mix well.
- Add the fixative, and gently shake or mix thoroughly.
- Add the fragrant oil, one drop at a time, mixing well between drops. (It is best to use an eye-dropper for this.)
- The pot pourri should now be covered and put aside in a cool, dark place such as a cupboard for about two weeks. (If you are using a paper bag, turn over the top of the bag and secure it with a clothes peg or paper

clip.) Two or three times a week give the mixture in the container a gentle shake or stir.

If you cannot bear to wait that long, you can use the pot pourri straight away, but the scent will not be mature, since it takes time for the various fragrances to blend properly.

- At the end of two weeks, give the mixture a final shake or stir and then smell the pot pourri to decide whether the scent is strong enough. If it is not, add some more oil, *one drop at a time.* Mix well between drops. Take care not to add too much oil. It is easy to add more if the perfume is too weak, but impossible to take it out if the scent is too strong.
- When you are satisfied with the perfume, put the pot pourri mix into decorative jars and pots.

A WORD OF WARNING

Fragrant oil will damage painted or varnished surfaces and will leave stains on fabric. Use it carefully. If you are storing your finished pot pourri in a paper bag or box, rest it on waxed paper or a large plate so that any oil seeping through will not do any damage.

Other simple recipes

To make these recipes, follow the same directions given in the basic recipe.

Rose Pot Pourri

about 4 cups dried rose petals
10 dried mint leaves, crumbled
10 cloves, crushed
½ cinnamon stick, crumbled
½ teaspoon ground allspice
1 cup crumbled oakmoss or 1 tablespoon orris root powder
10 drops of fragrant rose oil

Lavender Pot Pourri

about 3 cups dried lavender flowers
1 cup dried red rose petals and any dried blue or purple flower petals (for colour)
4 tablespoons dried mint leaves
2 tablespoons dried rosemary
1 cup crumbled oakmoss or 1 tablespoon orris root powder
10 drops of fragrant lavender oil

Rose and Lavender Pot Pourri

3 cups dried rose petals
1 cup dried lavender
¾ cup dried lemon verbena leaves
about ¼ cup dried marjoram
about ¼ cup dried rosemary
½ to 1 cup dried orange peel
2 tablespoons allspice
1 tablespoon crushed cloves
1½ cups crumbled oakmoss or 1½ tablespoons orris root powder
8 drops fragrant rose oil
2 drops lavender oil

Summertime Pot Pourri

2 cups dried rose petals
3 cups any red or blue-tinted petals or blossoms such as hydrangea, bougainvillea, salvia
2 cups dried orange peel
8 whole cloves, crushed
½ cinnamon stick, crumbled
1¼ cups crumbled oakmoss or 5 teaspoons orris root powder
4 drops eucalyptus oil
10 drops fragrant rose oil

Lemon-Scented Citrus Pot Pourri

2 cups dried lemon verbena leaves
dried peel of one lemon (small bits)
3 cups dried golden- or yellow-toned petals, such as marigold, nasturtiums, calendulas and yellow daisies
1¼ cups crumbled oakmoss or 5 teaspoons orris root powder
6 drops of fragrant lemon oil (such as lemon verbena or lemon-scented gum)

Golden Orange-Scented Pot Pourri

2 cups dried orange peel
1 cup of any other dried citrus peel (lemon, mandarin, lime, grapefruit)
1 cup dried orange blossoms
1 cup dried nasturtiums, calendulas, marigolds or any other orange or yellow flowers
½ cup each of dried orange mint and pineapple mint leaves (if these are unavailable, use 1 cup of ordinary mint)
1 cup crumbled oakmoss or 1 tablespoon orris root powder
5 drops fragrant orange blossom oil
5 drops of oil of bergamot

Fruity Peach Pot Pourri

3 cups any pink- and apricot-coloured dried flower petals
1 cup pale-green, dried leaves
1 cup crumbled oakmoss or 1 tablespoon orris root powder

some wood shavings dyed pink and apricot (optional)
chopped pieces of dried apricot (optional)
8 drops fragrant peach oil
peach stones

After placing this pot pourri into decorative pots, add three or four peach stones to the top for decoration.

Very Easy Australian Bush Pot Pourri

Lemon-scented leaves and eucalyptus oil combine to give this pot pourri a fresh, bushy scent.

2 cups of dried gum leaves
1 cup of any dried, lemon-scented bush leaves (such as lemon-scented eucalypts, bottlebrush, tea-tree or myrtle)
1 cup wattle flowers
8 whole cloves (crushed)
1 cup crumbled oakmoss or 1 tablespoon orris root powder
6 drops of eucalyptus oil

seed pods or whole, dried flowers

After you have placed this pot pourri into decorative pots, add a few interesting seed pods and whole, dried flowers such as everlasting daisies for decoration.

Spicy Bush Pot Pourri

2 to 3 cups dried bush leaves mixed with yellow-, orange- or red-toned flowers
1 cup small seed pods and bark broken into small pieces
2 sticks of banksia velvet, broken into pieces
8 whole cloves
1 cup crumbled oakmoss or 1 tablespoon orris root powder
10 drops any spicy fragrant oil

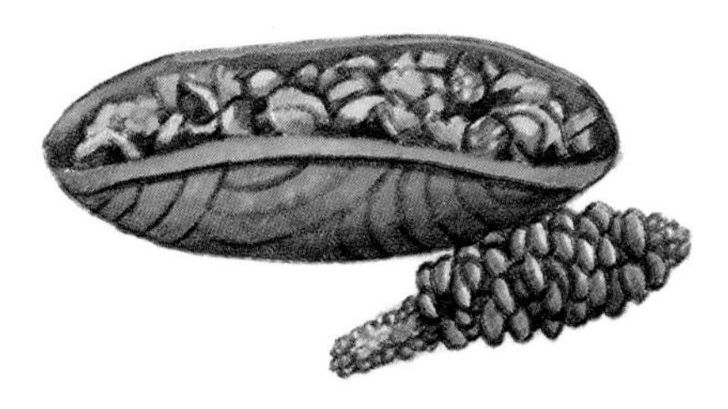

Rugged Spicy Pot Pourri

This pot pourri, made mostly from wood chips, cones, seed pods and wood shavings, is scented with any traditional spice fragrance. Because

of its heavily textured look and spicy smell, it is very suitable as a gift for men. If you want more colour, dye the wood shavings and cones with food colouring.

4 cups wood shavings, bush leaves, bark, small cones or seed pods and wood chips
2 cups yellow and orange dried flowers
1 cinnamon stick, broken into pieces
8 whole cloves
1½ cups crumbled oakmoss or 1½ tablespoons orris root powder
12 drops any spicy fragrant oil
pine cones or banksia velvet

After you have placed this pot pourri into decorative pots, add some small pine cones or banksia velvet for decoration.

HINT
Large pine cones painted with a spicy fragrant oil and placed in a bowl near the fire in winter will fill the room with a lovely scent.

Ocean Shores Pot Pourri
To make this pot pourri, first collect dried seaweed (or any dried plant that looks like seaweed), wood shavings, small pieces of

papery bark and fluffy seed heads. Colour them in various shades of blue, green and aqua with food colouring.

3 cups dried and dyed seaweed, wood shavings, papery bark and fluffy seed heads
1 cup dried blue flower petals
1 cup small pretty shells, especially those with a pearly finish
1 cup crumbled oakmoss or 1 tablespoon orris root powder
10 drops any sharp citrus fragrant oil

HINT
This pot pourri will look even more attractive if placed in a large shell, instead of an ordinary pot.

Quick and Easy Christmas Pot Pourri

4 cups red rose petals, or any dried red flower petals
2 cups dried green leaves
2 cups soft seed pods, small woody seed pods, cones and wood shavings dyed dark green
2 cups crumbled oakmoss or 2 tablespoons orris root powder
12 drops traditional spice fragrant oil
small amount of red and green glitter, if you like

When you are ready to use this pot pourri, sprinkle through green and red glitter (available from newsagents) and mix well. Put into open bowls decorated with small Christmas baubles or tinsel.

Pot Pourri Jars and Pots

As long as it is not metal or plastic, you can use almost any type of container for displaying your pot pourri. It does not need to have a lid.

Because pot pourris in the past were made to cover up smells, people made them in large amounts and stored them in large, lidded containers. Since people also wanted to make the scent last as long as possible, the lids were only taken off when the rooms were in use. Today, we make pot pourri because we *enjoy* the scent. So, let's enjoy it all the time. As the fragrance fades, add more oil, scented leaves and blossoms, or spices to freshen it up. Of course, you can cover your pot pourri when it is not in use, and the scent will last a little longer if you do.

A WORD OF WARNING

Remember that fragrant oil will damage painted or polished wooden furniture. If you are putting a pot pourri containing oil into an unglazed or wooden container, make sure you put some coins, or a saucer, under the bowl to keep it from coming in contact with the woodwork.

Where to find containers

The kitchen cupboard, grandma's old dresser, garage sales, white elephant stalls and op shops are great places to find suitable bowls and containers for pot pourri. You can use any of the following:

Attractively shaped jars, pots and wide-necked bottles
Sugar bowls
Jam and honey pots
Ginger jars
Sweets jars
China teapots and coffee pots
China kitchen canisters
Small woven cane or wicker baskets (these might need to be lined with paper to stop the mixture falling through)
Wooden bowls (remember that the scent — and oil, if you use it — will seep into wood, so don't use a wooden bowl if you want to reuse it for food later on)
Cardboard boxes (covered with attractive paper)
Cigar boxes or any other small wooden box. Wooden boxes, when filled with a spicy or wood scented pot pourri, make most attractive pot pourris
Large seashells
Large seed pods

Choosing the right container

Choose a container which matches the type of pot pourri you have made. Floral-scented and fruity pot pourris are best in pretty jars or fine china teapots and bowls, while citrus, spicy and woody pot pourris (containing cones, wood-shavings and seed pods) look great in simple containers such as plain crockery teapots, canisters, woven baskets, or wooden bowls and boxes.

Decorating the container

To decorate plain containers, tie a few dried flowers to the lid or handles using dried grasses or scraps of ribbon, or glue pressed flowers or leaves on the outside. Wooden boxes can be

made more interesting if you glue some pods or cones onto the lid or the sides of the box.

You could also give your pot pourri a finishing touch by adding one or two whole, dried flowers or cones to the top of the mix. For a floral pot pourri, try tiny rosebuds or everlasting daisies. For a bush or citrus mix, try small seed pods or whole, dried or pressed flowers, and for a spicy mix, experiment with small pine cones or perhaps some cinnamon bark.

To freshen or revive a pot pourri

After a while, the scent of all pot pourris will begin to fade. When this happens, simply add fresh spice or stir in three or four drops of

fragrant oil, and your pot pourri will be as good as new. Should the colour look a little dull, add a handful of newly dried leaves and blossoms to give it a lift. There is no such thing as an 'old' pot pourri!

If you are making pot pourris as gifts, always write the name of the spices or fragrant oil you have used on a small tag, so that the new owner will know what to add. The oil need not be the same as the one that was originally used, but should belong to the same family (see page 33).

Pomanders and Sachets

Pomanders

As you already know, people originally used pomanders to cover up body odour, keep away germs and disguise the smells in the street. We no longer need pomanders for these reasons, but we can use them to scent our cupboards and drawers.

One type of pomander we use today is a small hollow ball made of china which has several holes around its top — rather like the silver and gold pomanders of olden times. A fragrant mix of spices is placed inside the china

ball, which is then hung in a cupboard or placed in a drawer where it gives off perfume for a very long time.

If you have an old china pomander that has lost its scent, don't throw it away. You can revive it by adding either a couple of drops of fragrant oil, a teaspoon of cracked cloves and cinnamon, or by refilling it with your favourite pot pourri mixture.

A pomander which does not need a special container is the citrus pomander. As it is simply a dried, spiced citrus fruit it is easy, as well as fun, to make.

The citrus pomander was first used by Cardinal Wolsey about 500 years ago, in the time of King Henry the Eighth. The Cardinal,

who was head of the English church at the time, had to visit the sick as part of his work. To keep germs away and cover up the street smells, he always carried with him an orange which had been covered with sweet-smelling cloves.

How to make a citrus pomander

A WORD OF WARNING
Try not to use fruit from the fruit shop as it might have been waxed and will not dry out properly. Try to use fruit from the garden or bought from a roadside stall in the country.

What you need

a thin-skinned piece of citrus fruit (not too juicy), without any soft spots or marks
about 1 cup of whole cloves, with strong stems and large heads
1 dessertspoon ground cinnamon
1 dessertspoon orris root powder

What to do

- Using an old, fine knitting needle or a strong toothpick, prick a hole carefully in

the fruit and then press a clove firmly into the hole. Keep doing this until the skin of the fruit is completely covered with cloves. Since the fruit will shrink as it dries, the clove heads should not quite touch each other. (If you want to hang up the pomander, leave a 1 centimetre (½ inch) path free of cloves, so that you can more easily tie a ribbon around the finished pomander.)

- Place the fruit in a paper bag with the cinnamon and orris root powder. Close the top of the bag and shake well, until the fruit and cloves are completely covered with the mixture.
- Leave the fruit and the spice mixture in the bag in an airy place for one month, shaking the bag every day.
- At the end of a month, open the bag. The fruit, which should have dried out by this time, will feel hard and will have shrunk quite a bit.
- Shake off the spice mixture. The pomander is now ready to use. Either tie a pretty ribbon around it and hang it in a cupboard, or place it in a drawer.

The scent of this citrus pomander will last for years. When the fragrance does begin to fade, you can revive it by painting the pomander with oil of cloves or any other fragrant oil.

Sachets

A sachet is a small bag filled with a fragrant mixture of herbs, spices and flowers. Sachets can be small enough to hang on a coathanger, or large enough to use as a small pillow. Some, especially those which contain lavender, rosemary or citrus peel, will help repel moths. Others can be used to add a lovely herbal scent to bathwater. There are even sachets which can be used to keep fleas away from your pet dog or cat.

The first thing you must do is make the sachet bag. Although you can use any light material such as organdie, fine cotton, tulle or muslin, the easiest way to make a sachet bag is to use ordinary cotton handkerchiefs.

HINT

If you are using a fragrant oil mixture to fill your sachets check that it is not *too* oily, or else the oil could seep through the sachet and leave a stain.

Sleep sachets

Sleep sachets make a lovely gift. They are placed inside the pillowslip, between the pillowslip and the pillow itself. The warmth from the person's head releases the scent from the fragrant leaves and flowers while he or she sleeps.

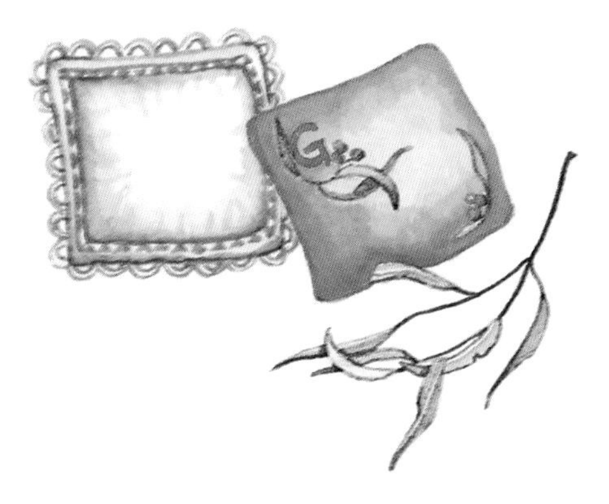

What to do

To make a sleep sachet, take two pretty handkerchiefs which are the same size. If you like, you can use plain hankies and decorate them with ribbons and scraps of lace, or draw your own design on them with fabric pens or crayons. If the sachet is for someone special, you might like to make a design using the person's initials.

When you are happy with the pattern, sew or glue the hankies together using craft glue on three sides. This will make a small bag. Fill

the bag loosely, with your favourite pot pourri or sachet mix, so that it is still fairly flat, and sew or glue up the opening.

Your sleep sachet is now ready to use.

Small clothing and linen sachets

These are usually smaller than sleep sachets but you can make them any size you like. Use them in your clothes drawers, or put them amongst the bedlinen or towels in the linen cupboard.

What to do

Before you begin, read the directions for making sleep sachets for tips on how to decorate plain hankies.

- Take a small handkerchief, or a square of fabric about the same size.
- Fold it in half, so the right sides are together, to make either a triangle or rectangle shape.
- Sew or join the sides together with craft glue, making sure you leave an opening big enough to put in the filling. Turn the bag right way out to hide the raw edges.
- Loosely fill the bag with your favourite pot pourri or one of the sachet mixtures.
- Sew up the opening, or, if you have chosen a rectangular shape, just tie a ribbon round the top.

Coathanger sachets
These sachets, which are quite small, are the easiest of all to make.

What to do

- Take a small, pretty handkerchief or cut out a square of material about 15 centimetres (6 inches) square. If the material you have chosen frays, it is best to use pinking shears (these leave a zig-zag edge) instead of scissors.

- In the middle of the square, put a small amount of your favourite pot pourri or sachet mixture.
- Gather the edges of the square into the middle and fasten tightly with a rubber band, so that the sachet mix is in a firm little ball.
- Tie a ribbon or scrap of lace over the band, making a loop or bow so that you can slip the sachet over the coathanger hook.

Herbal bath sachets

To make a herbal bath sachet, follow the directions for the coathanger sachet, but instead of filling it with a sachet mix, use ½ cup of either dried lemon verbena, rosemary, lavender

or mint. If you like, you could also try mixing two or three herbs together to make ½ cup mixture.

Herbs that go well together are: mint, rosemary and lemon balm; rosemary, sage and mint; and lavender and thyme.

Tie a ribbon around the sachet and hang it on the hot tap so that the water will run through it. When the bath has been run, squeeze the sachet out over the water. One sachet should be enough to scent two baths.

Special skin softening bath sachet

To make a bath sachet which also softens the skin, use ¼ cup of oatmeal mixed with ¼ cup

of herbs for each sachet. When the bath has been run, swish the sachet around in the water, squeeze it out several times and then use it as a bath mitt. Bath sachets containing oatmeal can be used only once.

Herb sachets on a rope

These are plaited wool or cord ropes with a number of small herbal sachets attached to them. They can be hung up in any room in the house, from a curtain rod or door handle, or any other convenient place.

What you need

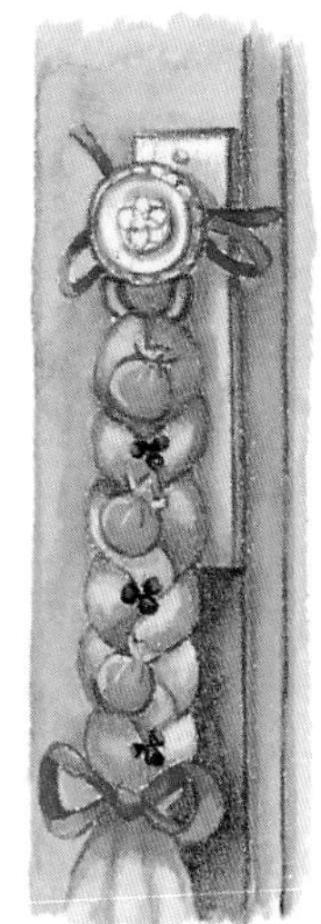

about 12 metres (36 feet) of thick wool or macrame cord cut into 12 one-metre (3 feet) pieces (You could also use 3 stockings or 3 pantyhose legs which have had the feet cut off.)

one wooden, metal or plastic curtain ring

four or five small coathanger sachets filled with herbs or spices

What to do

- Knot the wool, cord or pantyhose together at one end.
- Attach this end to the curtain ring, either by tying it around the ring, or sewing the ring onto it.
- Hook the ring over something firm, such as a hook or door handle.
- Divide the wool, cord or pantyhose into three even bundles and plait them into a thick rope.
- When you come to the end of the plait, tie the loose ends together firmly with a ribbon.
- Attach your herb sachets evenly along the plait by sewing or tying them into place.

Your plait is now ready to hang up. For extra decoration, you could push a few pieces of cinnamon stick, banksia velvet or interesting seed pods into the plait.

Flower and herb sacks

These are similar to sleep or linen sachets but instead of being put into cupboards or drawers they are hung by a ribbon in a handy spot so that every time you go past you can give the sack a squeeze. This will release the fragrance into the room.

For bedrooms and living rooms, make the bags from scraps of pretty fabric or handkerchiefs, following the directions on pages 57–8 for sachets. Fill them loosely with a pot pourri or sachet mix and tie them with ribbon to the bedhead, curtain rails or backs of chairs.

For the kitchen, make a hessian or checked gingham bag and fill it with a sharp herb mixture (see pages 20–1). The scent will help cover up cooking smells and keep flies away.

Pet sachets

To make a sachet which will help keep fleas away from your pet dog or cat, fill a small cloth bag, or old sock with any insect repelling herb, such as lavender, rosemary, or mint. Place the sachet under the pet's bedding. When the sachet loses it scent, replace the mixture.

Cat toy

You can also recycle an old sock to make a toy mouse for your cat. Stuff it with dried cat mint, and your cat will find it hard to resist.

- Take an old, small sock.
- In the middle of the toe-end of the sock, pinch the material into a small bubble shape to make a nose. Tie this in place by winding wool or cotton around the base of the 'nose' and knotting it firmly.

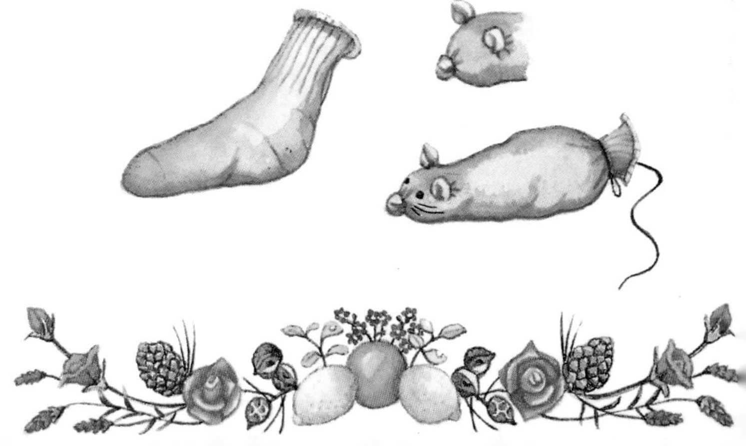

- Pinch up two ear shapes above the nose and tie them in place with a piece of wool or ribbon.
- Stuff the sock with dried catnip or catmint.
- Tie a piece of wool or cord firmly around the open end of the sock to stop the catnip falling out, and leave a length of the wool or cord dangling for the tail.
- With marking pens, draw on some whiskers and two eyes.

Instead of making a mouse, you could make a catnip sachet for your cat's favourite sleeping place, or use an old sock to make a catnip ball.

Some simple recipes for filling sachets

These recipes, only one of which uses a fragrant oil, can also be used for pot pourris. The amounts given will fill one or two larger sachets and a number of small ones.

Lemon Verbena Sachet

Fill sachet with dried lemon verbena.

Old-Fashioned Lavender Sachet

Fill the sachet with dried lavender and a few crushed cloves. If the scent is not strong enough, add a little fragrant lavender oil.

Rosemary and Lemon Sachet

½ cup dried rosemary
1 cup dried lemon verbena
about 20 dried mint leaves
dried peel of 1 lemon

Mix well and fill sachets.

Rosemary and Herb Sachet

½ cup dried rosemary
½ cup dried lemon verbena
1 cup dried pine needles

Crush the leaves to help release the scent. Mix well and fill sachets.

Rose and Lavender Sachet

½ cup dried fragrant rose petals
½ cup dried lavender
¼ cup dried thyme or dried lemon verbena
1 small stick of crushed cinnamon or 10 crushed cloves

Mix well before putting into sachets.

Fresh and Minty Sachet

Take ¼ cup each of dried mint, lemon verbena, lemon balm and rose petals

Mix well and fill sachets.

Rosemary and Lavender Sachet

½ cup dried lavender
½ cup dried rosemary
some dried orange peel
about 10 whole cloves

Mix well and place in sachets.

Herb and Lemon Sachet

¼ cup each of dried lavender, thyme and lemon balm

Mix well and place in sachets.

Australian Bush Sachet

Mix 1 cup any dried eucalyptus leaves with ½ cup any dried, lemon-scented bush leaves

Place in sachets.

Fragrant Floral Sachet

1 cup mixed, scented dried flower petals
½ cup dried lavender
½ cup dried lemon verbena
½ cup dried rosemary
½ cup dried orange peel
2 or 3 drops of fragrant orange or bergamot oil

Mix well and place in sachets.

Other Nice-Smelling Things

Herbal vinegars

Bottles of delicately flavoured vinegars and salad oils make a most welcome and original gift for all those who like to cook.

What you need

a clean glass bottle, with a lid or cork
enough good white vinegar or good cooking oil to almost fill the bottle
three or four large sprigs of fresh *herbs, such as oregano, basil, dill, tarragon, rosemary, mint, thyme, or a few cloves of peeled garlic*
a fine kitchen strainer
a large jug or mixing bowl
a funnel

What to do

- Pour the vinegar or oil into the empty bottle.
- Add the herbs and put on the lid or cork.
- Give the bottle a shake and place it in a warm place, such as a window sill or near the hot water system, for about a week.

- After a week, pour the oil or vinegar through the strainer and into the jug or bowl. Throw away the herbs.
- Using the funnel, carefully pour the oil or vinegar back into the bottle.
- Push two or three fresh sprigs of herbs into the bottle and reseal.

The vinegar or oil is now ready to use in salads or cooking.

HINT

Herbal vinegar can also be used in the bathroom. For a refreshing bath, just add a cupful of herbal vinegar to the bathwater.

Scented bath oils

It requires a bit more effort to turn ordinary cooking oil into beautifully scented bath oil. As you will need quite a lot of petals or herbs to give the oil a really strong scent, try making only a small amount to begin with. When making this bath oil it is best to use a light oil, such as light olive oil or safflower oil, which doesn't have a scent of its own.

What you need

a glazed mixing bowl
any clean, empty bottle with a lid or cork
enough cooking oil to fill the bottle
a quantity of highly scented rose petals or very fragrant herbs, such as rosemary leaves and lavender flowers
an old plate to cover the bowl

What to do

- Tip the oil into the bowl.
- Add the petals or herbs until you cannot fit any more into the oil.
- Place the plate on top of the bowl and then put the bowl in the sun for two days.
- Remove the petals or herbs and squeeze them thoroughly into the oil, before throwing them away.
- Fill the bowl with more petals or herbs and leave in the sun for another two days before repeating the last step. (If the scent is not strong enough, repeat the last two steps until you are satisfied.)
- Pour the oil into the bottle and decorate it with ribbon or dried flowers. One or two capsful will scent the bath and your skin. If you don't want to bathe in oily water, you can rub a tiny amount of oil into your skin after your bath.

HINT

If you want to make your own bath oil but do not have enough scented flowers you can simply add fragrant oil to the cooking oil.

Scented notepaper

By using your favourite pot pourri or sachet mix, you can turn ordinary notepaper into beautifully scented stationery.

What you need

a box of unscented notepaper and envelopes
a small amount of pot pourri or sachet mix placed inside an envelope or small, flat sachet

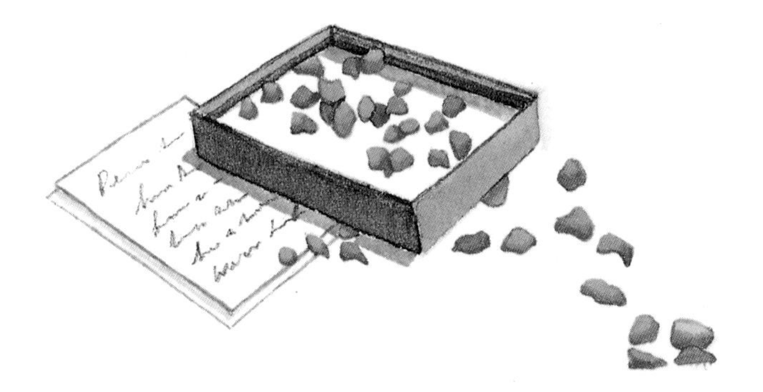

What to do

- Place the envelope or sachet inside the box of notepaper. If there is fragrant oil in your pot pourri mixture, make sure that it does not stain the notepaper.

- Put the lid on the box and put it aside for at least a week.
- Remove the sachet.

Your notepaper will now be scented. If you wish to give it as a present, scatter a few dried rose petals over the top of the notepaper paper before giftwrapping the box in pretty paper.

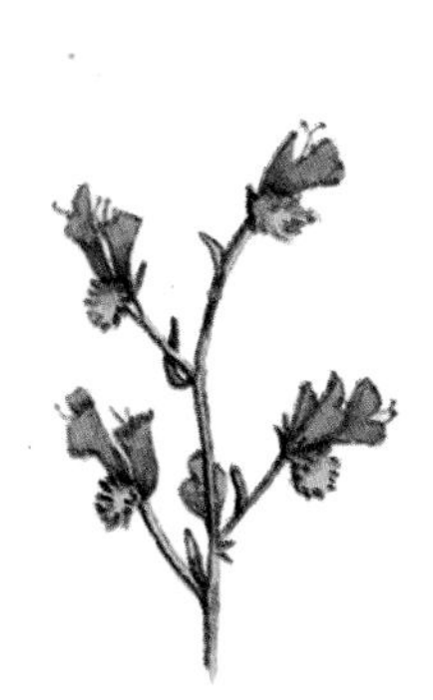